Great Artists
of the World

Rembrandt van Rijn

Alix Wood

W
FRANKLIN WATTS
LONDON • SYDNEY

Franklin Watts

First published in Great Britain in 2015 by the Watts Publishing Group

Copyright © Alix Wood Books
Produced for Franklin Watts by Alix Wood Books www.alixwoodbooks.co.uk

Editor: Eloise Macgregor
Designer: Alix Wood

Photo Credits: Cover, 1 © nga/Andrew W. Mellon Collection; 4, 9, 16-17, 29 © nga/Rosenwald Collection; 3, 5 top, 29 top © Shutterstock; 5 bottom © frog in the pond; 6 © Oleg Golovnev/Shutterstock; 7 © National Museum, Stockholm; 8, 15, 18 © Rijksmuseum, Amsterdam; 11, 19, 21 © nga/Widener Collection; 12 National Gallery, London; 13, 26 © Gemäldegalerie, Berlin; 14 © Jaroslav Moravcik/Shutterstock; 22-23 © John Paul Getty Museum; 25 © Isabella Stewart Gardner Museum, Boston; 27 © Harmenz van Rijn Kremer Collection; 28 © Voytikof

Dewey number 709

ISBN 978 1 4451 4422 1

Library eBook ISBN 978 1 4451 4423 8

Printed in China

Franklin Watts
An imprint of
Hachette Children's Group
Part of The Watts Publishing Group
Carmelite House
50 Victoria Embankment
London EC4Y 0DZ

An Hachette UK Company

www.hachette.co.uk

www.franklinwatts.co.uk

Contents

Who Was Rembrandt?

Rembrandt is one of the most important painters and etchers in art history. He is particularly famous for his portraits and **self-portraits**. His paintings are rich in colour and use dramatic areas of light and shade.

Rembrandt's self-portrait, aged 24

Map of the World

North America

Europe

Asia

Africa

South America

Australia

NETHERLANDS

Rembrandt was born in 1606 in Leiden, the Netherlands. His full name was Rembrandt Harmenszoon van Rijn. He was his parents' ninth child! His father was a miller and his mother was a baker's daughter.

A windmill in Leiden, the Netherlands

Early Education

The Latin School, Leiden

Rembrandt's parents made sure he got a good education. After primary school, at age 10, Rembrandt was sent to the Latin School in Leiden. He took bible study classes and lessons in "the classics". The classics included subjects such as Latin and Greek. At the age of 14 Rembrandt enrolled at the University of Leiden. He did not stay there for long, though.

Studying Art

University life did not suit Rembrandt and he left to study art. He studied with the painter Jacob van Swanenburgh for around three years. Van Swanenburgh liked to paint scenes of hell and the underworld. He painted fire and its reflections on objects. Rembrandt often painted reflections in his later work, too.

Rembrandt left Leiden and headed for the Dutch capital, Amsterdam. He became a pupil of Pieter Lastman, a well-known painter who placed figures from the bible, and from history, into his **landscapes**. Rembrandt adopted this style in later life, too.

David's Farewell to Jonathan,
Rembrandt, 1642

Self-Portrait, 1630. Rembrandt is aged around 24 here

Young Success

Rembrandt opened a studio in Leiden around 1624 with a colleague, Jan Lievens. He would have been just 18 or 19 years old. Lievens had achieved success at an even younger age. Lievens went as an **apprentice** to Pieter Lastman in Amsterdam at around the age of 10. At around 12 years old Lievens began a career as an independent artist!

Teaching Art

Rembrandt started teaching students himself at the age of 22. As his fame grew many young artists wanted to learn from him. It is thought that, over his lifetime, Rembrandt had around fifty students who studied with him. Much of the work of Rembrandt's students resembled his paintings very closely. This caused confusion, especially as Rembrandt signed his assistants' works as his own!

Blessing of Jacob 1638, is by Govert Flinck, one of Rembrandt's students

Rembrandt and his pupils sketched the same models and landscapes side by side. They would draw the same farm buildings but from different angles. At first the drawings were all thought to be by Rembrandt himself.

Landscape with a Cottage and a Large Tree, 1641, by Rembrandt

Having students meant that Rembrandt earned money. The students would pay for **tuition** and Rembrandt also made some money from selling their paintings.

Coin Trick

Rembrandt's students became very good artists, and good tricksters. Students would paint coins on the studio floor which Rembrandt would try and pick up.

Light and Dark

Rembrandt liked to experiment with light and dark in his paintings. This effect is called *chiaroscuro*. The term comes from Italian, "chiaro" means clear, and "oscuro" means dark. Rembrandt learned this technique by studying paintings by Leonardo da Vinci and Caravaggio.

Rembrandt's paintings used strong **contrasts**. His use of light and shadow created exciting atmospheres for his figures. Rembrandt often painted the eyes in an area of shadow. This helped make the subject of his painting look mysterious and thoughtful.

Lights!

By adding light to an otherwise dark painting, Rembrandt could focus the viewer onto the lit area. The effect is a little like putting a spotlight on an actor on stage! In the film industry, the term "Rembrandt lighting" is still used today to mean one light source which creates sharp contrasts between light and shadow.

Portrait of a Gentleman with a Tall Hat and Gloves, around 1659

Self-Portraits

Rembrandt created around one hundred self-portraits! Most of these were paintings but he also did thirty-two **etchings** and seven drawings. Why did he paint so many? And why was he often wearing strange clothes or pulling faces?

Many of his self-portraits were **tronies**. Tronies are head-and-shoulder portraits. The model is dressed playing a role, such as being a milkmaid, or expressing an emotion. Tronies were very popular in the Netherlands at the time. Artists also painted tronies to practice different expressions for their other paintings.

Self-portrait, 1640. Many self-portraits show Rembrandt in costume.

Self-portrait in a Velvet Beret, 1634

The Night Watch

Rembrandt's most famous painting became known as *The Night Watch*. It was orginally called *The Militia Company of Captain Frans Banning Cocq*. The painting became so dirty over time that it looked like a night scene. Once cleaned, it became clear that the painting was set in daylight after all!

The Night Watch is an enormous painting. It was originally even larger. Amsterdam Town Hall cut around 20 per cent of the canvas away so that it would fit on their wall!

An Action Portrait

When the Captain asked Rembrandt to paint his company's portrait, he was probably expecting a painting of a line of men. Instead he got one of the most exciting military portraits in history. Rembrandt used light areas to pick out the most important men in the guards. There is a lot happening in this painting. Can you see a little girl with a dead chicken tied to her belt?

Etchings

Rembrandt was more famous during his lifetime for his etchings than for his paintings. An etching is made by coating a metal plate with beeswax. The design is drawn into the wax with a sharp tool. Acid then eats away the areas unprotected by the beeswax. The plate is then covered in ink and used to make a print.

Rembrandt sometimes took several years to finish a plate to his satisfaction. He sometimes sold prints from different stages of the plate's progress. By the 1650s customers came from as far south as Italy to collect his work! The etching *Christ Preaching* shows his incredible skill. He used rich dark detail in some areas of the pictures.

The Hundred Guilder Print

This etching is also called "The Hundred Guilder Print". This was how much money Rembrandt's customers paid for it. That was a lot of money. The Dutch bought Manhattan Island in New York at around the same time for 60 guilders.

Christ Preaching, 1649

Rembrandt's Family

Rembrandt married Saskia van Uylenburgh, the cousin of a successful art dealer. She helped his career by introducing him to wealthy people who commissioned portraits. They had four children, but only the last, a boy named Titus, survived. Saskia died aged 30 leaving Rembrandt to bring up the boy.

Titus

Rembrandt painted several portraits of his son. He was often wearing costume, in this portrait he is dressed as a monk! Titus would have been aged 19 when this was painted.

Titus as a Monk, 1660

Rembrandt probably began this portrait of Saskia shortly after their marriage in 1634. It took him until 1639 to be happy with it! **X-ray** images of the painting have shown that the shawl and neck collar were added later to the painting.

Saskia van Uylenburgh, Rembrandt's wife, painted around 1639

Looking Natural

Rembrandt had a great reputation as a portrait painter during his lifetime. His portraits were much livelier and more natural than those of other portrait painters at the time. Modern techniques which track people's eye movements while looking at a painting show why people find his work so appealing. Rembrandt's light and dark **technique** guides people's eyes around the painting in a pleasing way. Where do your eyes go first when you look at this painting?

A Pair of Paintings?

It is believed that *Portrait of a Lady with an Ostrich-feather Fan* is part of a pair of paintings. The other painting is the *Portrait of a Gentleman with a Tall Hat and Gloves* on page 11. Why do people think that? The paintings were kept together in a collection for many years. Their poses are very similar to other pairs of portraits done by other Dutch painters. No one is too sure who the sitters are.

Portrait of a Lady with an Ostrich-Feather Fan, around 1659

Painting a Story

Rembrandt painted several large, dramatic paintings inspired by stories from the Bible or from history. This painting tells the story of the god Jupiter, who disguised himself as a white bull in order to take the princess Europa away with him across the sea.

Rembrandt painted the picture for Jacques Specx, an important Dutch merchant. Rembrandt may have added modern details such as the crane in the background to connect the story to Specx's own life.

The Abduction of Europa, 1632

Bible Stories

Rembrandt painted many stories from the Bible. *The Storm on the Sea of Galilee* tells the story from the gospel of Mark, about how Jesus calmed the stormy waves. It is Rembrandt's only seascape.

In March 1990, *The Storm on the Sea of Galilee* and several other works were stolen from a Boston museum by thieves disguised as police officers. The museum still displays the paintings' empty frames in their place.

Rembrandt's paintings have been stolen before. A Rembrandt portrait of Jacob de Gheyn III has been stolen four times since 1966! It earned the name the "takeaway Rembrandt" and a place in the *Guinness Book of World Records*!

Look Familiar?

Look closely at the man in blue in the centre of the boat looking straight at you. Rembrandt liked to paint himself in many of his bible story paintings.

The Storm on the Sea of Galilee, 1633

Is it a Rembrandt?

Many works originally thought to be by Rembrandt were actually not. Some were done by his students and some by other artists. Confusingly, Rembrandt signed his work in several different ways and even with different spellings!

Rembrant Rembrandt

Man in a Golden Helmet, 1650, is one of the most famous portraits no longer believed to be by Rembrandt.

Art historians use modern **forensic** techniques to study paintings. They test the paint and the board. They x-ray for drawings beneath the paint. Many paintings that were thought to be by Rembrandt have been **discredited**. Some new works have been **credited**.

The painting *Old Man With a Turban* was originally thought to be by Rembrandt. An expert then decided that it was not, and the painting was stored in a museum basement. Rembrandt experts have now accepted that it is actually by Rembrandt.

The Real Jesus!

Sometimes confusion was caused because of sloppy catalogue entries. In 1656, Rembrandt wished to sell several paintings to pay off debts. One painting was listed in the catalogue as being "Head of Christ, done from life". As Christ wouldn't have been alive then it seems unlikely!

Rembrandt's legacy

Rembrandt died in 1669 in Amsterdam. He was one of the greatest painters and etchers ever to have lived. Even though he was very successful during his lifetime, he overspent, and had money troubles for much of his life. His son Titus had to sell most of his paintings to pay off his debts.

The house in which Rembrandt and Saskia lived in Amsterdam has became the Rembrandt House Museum. Rembrandt became bankrupt in 1656 while at the house and had to auction many of his belongings. The auction list helped the museum **reconstruct** how the house would have looked while he lived there.

The Rembrandt House Museum, Amsterdam

Statues

In celebration of the artist's 400th birthday, two Russian artists created statues of the famous painting *The Night Watch* around Rembrandt's statue in a square in Amsterdam. *The Night Watch* statues toured the world for three years but have now returned.

Rembrandt and *The Night Watch* statues in Amsterdam

The Artist's Mother, 1631

Rembrandt will be remembered not only for his paintings and etchings but also for his teaching workshops. Many of his students became accomplished and collected artists.

Glossary

apprentice
A person who is learning a trade or art by experience under a skilled worker.

contrasts
Differences in colour or brightness between things.

credited
To be thought of as the creator of a work.

discredited
To no longer be thought of as the creator of a work.

etchings
Prints made from an etched metal plate.

forensic
Scientific tests or techniques, often used in connection with the detection of crime.

landscapes
Pictures of natural scenery.

reconstruct
To construct again the same as before.

self-portraits
Portraits of oneself made by oneself.

technique
A method of achieving a desired aim.

tronies
Paintings of a head and shoulders featuring an exaggerated expression or an interesting character.

tuition
Money paid for instruction.

x-ray
Electromagnetic radiation that is able to penetrate solids and to photograph what is beneath.

Websites

A Kidskonnect site with information and useful links
https://kidskonnect.com/people/rembrandt-van-rijn/

Click on the Rembrandt portrait and learn about his paintings
http://www.nga.gov/education/timetravel/

Read More

Spence, David. *Rembrandt* (TickTock Essential Artists), London: TickTock Books, 2009.

Venezia, Mike. *Rembrandt* (Getting to Know the World's Greatest Artists). London, UK: Franklin Watts, 2015.

Woodhouse, Jayne. *The Life and Work of Rembrandt van Rijn.* London, UK: Heinemann Library, 2002.

Index